Greg Byrd, Lynn Byrd and Chris Pearce

Cambridge Checkpoint
Mathematics

Challenge Workbook

8

CAMBRIDGE
UNIVERSITY PRESS

CAMBRIDGE
UNIVERSITY PRESS

University Printing House, Cambridge CB2 8BS, United Kingdom

One Liberty Plaza, 20th Floor, New York, NY 10006, USA

477 Williamstown Road, Port Melbourne, VIC 3207, Australia

4843/24, 2nd Floor, Ansari Road, Daryaganj, Delhi – 110002, India

79 Anson Road, #06–04/06, Singapore 079906

Cambridge University Press is part of the University of Cambridge.

It furthers the University's mission by disseminating knowledge in the pursuit of
education, learning and research at the highest international levels of excellence.

www.cambridge.org
Information on this title: www.cambridge.org / 9781316637425 (Paperback)

First published 2017

20 19 18 17 16 15 14 13 12 11 10 9 8 7

Printed in Great Britain by CPI Group (UK) Ltd, Croydon CR0 4YY

A catalogue record for this publication is available from the British Library

ISBN 978-1-316-63742-5 Paperback

Contents

Introduction

Welcome to Cambridge Checkpoint Mathematics Challenge Workbook 8

The *Cambridge Checkpoint Mathematics* course covers the Cambridge Secondary 1 Mathematics curriculum framework. The course is divided into three stages: 7, 8 and 9.

You can use this Challenge Workbook with Coursebook 8 and Practice Book 8. It gives you increasingly more difficult tasks or presents you with alternative approaches or methods in order to build on your existing skills.

Like the Coursebook and the Practice Book, this Workbook is divided into 18 units. In each unit there are exercises on each topic that will develop and extend your skills and understanding in mathematics. This will improve and deepen your understanding of the units. At the end of each unit is a 'final challenge' to help you check your knowledge and understanding.

If you get stuck with a task:

- Read the question again.

- Think carefully about what you already know AND how you can use it in the answer.

- Read through the matching section in the Coursebook.

1.1 Multiples and factors

Here is a way to find the HCF and LCM of two numbers: 960 and 1680.

Write down the numbers. Find a common

factor, e.g. 10, and divide by it:

| 10 | 960 | 1680 |

Do the same thing with 96 and 168, e.g. 4:

| 4 | 96 | 168 |

Do the same thing with 24 and 42, e.g. 6:

| 6 | 24 | 42 |

4 and 7 have no common factor except 1.

Stop here.

                                                  4   7

Multiply the numbers on the left to find the HCF: $10 \times 4 \times 6 = 240$

Multiply the numbers on the left and on the bottom to find the LCM: $10 \times 4 \times 6 \times 4 \times 7 = 6720$

---

1   Use this method to find the HCF and LCM of 840 and 1260. This time start with 20.

Add more rows if you need to.

| 20 | 840 | 1260 |

| | 42 | 63 |

| | | |

HCF = ...

LCM = ...

---

2 Use the same method to find the HCF and LCM of 900 and 1260.

HCF = ...

LCM = ...

3 Use the same method to find the HCF and LCM of 864 and 1440.

HCF = ...

LCM = ...

4 Use the same method to find the HCF and LCM of 616 and 952.

HCF = ...

LCM = ...

5 Adapt the method to find the HCF and LCM of 90, 120 and 135.

HCF = ...

LCM = ...

6 Find the HCF and LCM of 840, 480 and 600.

HCF = ...

LCM = ...

1.2 Powers and roots

1 Look at these statements. Circle TRUE or FALSE for each one.

Give a reason for your answer.

a If N is odd, then $N^2 + 1$ is even.   TRUE   FALSE

Reason: ....

....

b If N is even, then $N^2 + 1$ is a prime number.   TRUE   FALSE

Reason: ....

....

2 Use a calculator to check that these statements are correct.

Fill in the missing number.

$1^3 = 1^2 = 1$

$4^3 = 8^2 = 64$

$9^3 = 27^2 = \ldots\ldots$

Write down some more numbers to continue the sequence.

....

....

Mixed questions

1

There are 20 teeth on the large cog and 12 teeth on the small one.

When the large cog makes A complete rotations, the small cog makes B complete rotations.

Find the smallest possible positive values of A and B.

....

....

A = ... B = ...

2

These cogs have 12, 25 and 18 teeth.

a The smallest cog (12 teeth) goes round clockwise.

Which way does the middle-sized cog (18 teeth) go round? ....

b The smallest cog goes round N whole turns.

The middle-sized cog goes round a whole number of turns.

Find the possible values of N. ....

c The smallest cog goes round M whole turns.

The largest cog (25 teeth) goes round a whole number of turns.

Find the possible values of M. ....

d Suppose the largest cog has 28 teeth.

What is the answer to b) in this case? ....

3 A number is semi-prime if it is the product of two different prime numbers.

For example, $21 = 3 \times 7$, so 21 is semi-prime.

a How many numbers less than 100 are semi-prime?

....

....

b What is the smallest number bigger than 1000 that is semi-prime?

....

This is a magic square.

10	5	6
3	7	11
8	9	4

The total of every row, column and diagonal is the same.

In the example above, the total is always 21.

4 Complete these magic squares.

a

2	−5	0
	−1	

b

4		
−3	2	1

c

		−1
	−3	1
−5		

5 **a** The product of two numbers is −24.

The difference between the two numbers is 11.

Find the numbers.

....

....

b The product of three numbers is 24.

The sum of the three numbers is 4.

Find the numbers.

....

....

2 Sequences, expressions and formulae

2.1 Generating sequences

1 Use the position-to-term rule to work out the first four terms of each sequence.

a term = (position number)^2 ....

....

b term = 2 × (position number)^2 ....

....

c term = (position number)^2 – 5 ....

....

d term = 10 × (position number)^2 – 10 ....

....

2 The sixth term of a sequence is 5. The tenth term is 7.

Which of these position-to-term rules is the correct one for the sequence?

A term = position number – 1

B term = 2 × position number – 7

C term = $\frac{1}{2}$ × position number + 2

D term = $\frac{1}{6}$ × position number + 4

....

....

2.2 Finding rules for sequences

1 This pattern is made from grey and white squares.

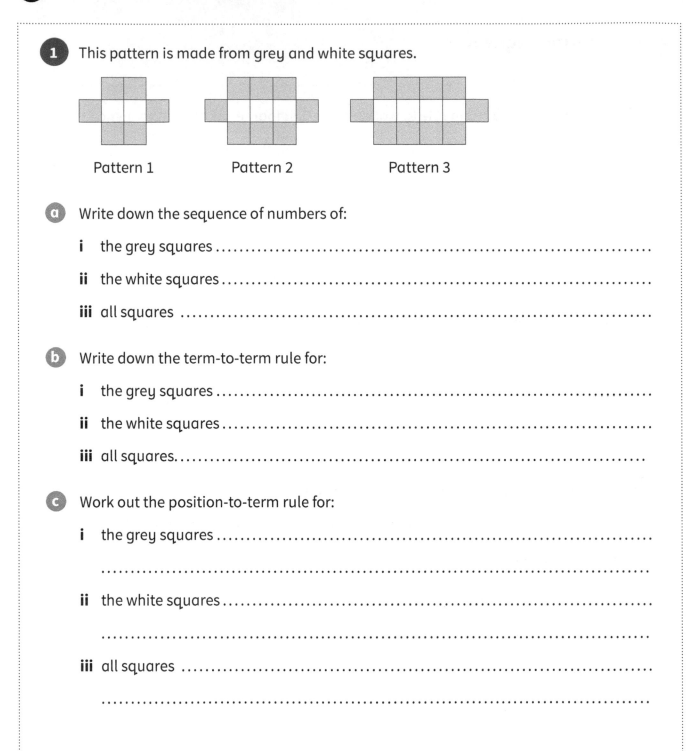

Pattern 1   Pattern 2   Pattern 3

a Write down the sequence of numbers of:

i the grey squares ....

ii the white squares ....

iii all squares ....

b Write down the term-to-term rule for:

i the grey squares ....

ii the white squares ....

iii all squares..

c Work out the position-to-term rule for:

i the grey squares ....

....

ii the white squares ....

....

iii all squares ....

....

2.3 Using the nth term

1 Work out the first three terms and the tenth term of these sequences with the given nth term.

a $\frac{1}{2}n$ ....

....

b n^2 ....

....

c $n^2 + \frac{1}{2}n + 1$ ....

....

2 The fifth term of a sequence is 4. The sixth term is 15.

Which of these nth term rules is the correct one for the sequence?

A $n - 1$ **B** $\frac{1}{5}n + 3$ **C** $n^2 - 21$ **D** $\frac{1}{2}n + 21$

....

....

....

....

....

2.4 Using functions and mappings

1 Work out the equation for this function machine.

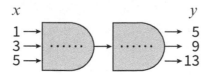

Explain how you worked out your answer.

....

....

....

....

2 Work out the equations for these function machines.

a
x y

$2 \rightarrow$ ..... $\rightarrow 4$
$3 \rightarrow$ ..... $\rightarrow 9$
$4 \rightarrow$ ..... $\rightarrow 16$

....

....

....

....

b
x y

$2 \rightarrow$ ..... $\rightarrow$ ..... $\rightarrow 5$
$3 \rightarrow$ ..... $\rightarrow$ ..... $\rightarrow 10$
$4 \rightarrow$ ..... $\rightarrow$ ..... $\rightarrow 17$

....

....

....

....

2.5 Constructing linear expressions

1 **a** Draw a line linking the description on the left with the correct expression on the right.

I think of a number, multiply it by 2 then subtract the result from 6.		$6n - 2$
		$2n + 6$
I think of a number, divide it by 6 then subtract the result from 2.		$6 - 2n$
		$2(n + 6)$
I think of a number, multiply it by 2 then add the result to 6.		$2 - \dfrac{n}{6}$

b There are two expressions left. Write a description for each one.

....

....

....

....

....

....

2.6 Deriving and using formulae

1 When $x = -4$, all these expressions except one have the same value.

Which is the odd one out?

| $x^2 - 7$ | $(x + 1)^2$ | $-\dfrac{36}{x}$ | $x - 5$ | $2x + 17$ | $5 - x$ |

....

....

....

2 Write down any values of x that make these pairs of expressions equal.

a $3x + 1$ and $3x^2 + 1$ ....

b $4 - x$ and $x - 4$ ....

c $\dfrac{5x}{2} + 5$ and $\dfrac{2x}{5} + 5$ ....

d $3(x + 2)$ and $2(x + 3)$ ....

Mixed questions

1 This pattern is made from dots.

Pattern 1   Pattern 2   Pattern 3   Pattern 4

a Draw the next pattern in the sequence.

b Explain how the sequence is formed.

....

c Complete the table.

Position number	1	2	3	4
Term	2	5		

d Write down the position-to-term rule.

i in words ....

ii using the nth term ....

e Complete the function machine for this sequence.

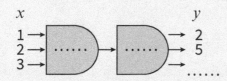

f Write the function machine in part e) as an equation ....

g How many dots will be in the tenth term? ....

2 The formula below is used to calculate the distance travelled by an object.

$s = ut + \dfrac{1}{2}at^2$ where: s = distance

u = starting speed

a = acceleration

t = time

Hint: $\dfrac{1}{2}at^2$ means $\dfrac{1}{2} \times a \times t^2$

Work out the distance travelled by an object when:

a $u = 0$, $a = 6$ and $t = 5$

....

....

b $u = 30$, $a = -4$ and $t = 10$

....

....

3 Place value, ordering and rounding

3.1 Multiplying and dividing by 0.1 and 0.01

1 Sid is a mathematical snake. Use the numbers and symbols from the box below to complete the workings on the snake. You can only use each number or symbol once. The numbers go on the dotted lines and the symbols go in the boxes.

| 0.1 | 0.5 | 100 | 50 | ÷ | 0.01 | 100 | × | 0.1 | 0.05 |

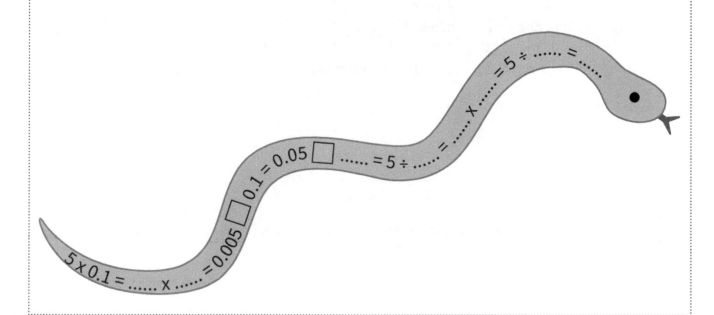

3.2 Ordering decimals

1 Write these decimal numbers in order of size, starting with the smallest.

a −4.2, −7.8, −3.6, −9.8, −1.4 ....

b −2.7, −2.1, −2.9, −2.5, −2.0 ....

c −1.6, −1.09, −1, −1.82, −1.4 ....

2 These are the fastest lap times for six motorcyclists during race qualification.

Motorcyclist	Time (min:sec)	Names in order, fastest first
Thulani Bopoto	2:28.666	
Pierre Duval	2:28.016	
Jettrin Juntasa	2:29.010	
Amir Khan	2:28.410	
Bernie Matthews	2:29.101	
Carlos Sanchez	2:29.007	

In the table, write the motorcyclists in order, starting with the fastest.

3.3 Rounding

1 Use a calculator to work out these fractions as decimals. Round each answer to 2 d.p.

a $\dfrac{1}{7}$ ....

b $\dfrac{5}{9}$ ....

2 Write down a number with 3 decimal places that rounds to:

a 5 to the nearest whole number and 5.5 to the nearest tenth ....

b 5 to the nearest whole number and 5.50 to the nearest hundredth ....

3.4 Adding and subtracting decimals

1 Work out:

a 500 – 2 = ...

b 500 – 2.4 = ...

c 500 – 2.45 = ...

d 500 – 2.456 = ...

2 In an 800 m race, runners do two laps of a track. These are the lap times of three 800 m runners.

Name	Lap 1 – 1st 400 m time (min:sec)	Lap 2 – 2nd 400 m time (min:sec)	Total time for 800 m (min:sec)
A. Patsun	1:12.45	1:18.36	
T. Nmobi	1:15.23	1:16.55	
S. Beach	1:16.01	1:13.12	

What is the difference in the total time taken to run 800 m between the fastest and slowest runners?

Use the last column in the table to help if you need to.

....

....

....

....

....

....

....

....

....

3.5 Dividing decimals

1 Three friends decide to share equally the cost of a meal. This is what they order:

Chicken balti $8.99

Vegetable korma $8.49

Prawn madras $10.25

a Work out how much they each pay. Round your answer to the nearest cent.

....

....

....

b If each of the friends pays the amount you calculated in part a), will the bill be paid in full? Explain your answer.

....

....

....

3.6 Multiplying by decimals

1 **a** Use the fact that $0.94 \times 7.3 = 6.862$ to work out:

   i $0.094 \times 7.3 =$ ....

   ii $0.94 \times 73 =$ ....

   iii $9.4 \times 0.73 =$ ....

b Write down one other multiplication that has an answer of 6.862.

....

2 Wayne changes £90 into US dollars ($) when the exchange rate is £1 = $1.41.

How many dollars does he get?

....

....

3 Work out:

a 0.4 × 0.4 = ...

b 0.03 × 0.07 = ...

c 0.1 × 0.06 = ...

d 0.09 × 0.5 = ...

3.7 Dividing by decimals

1 **a** Continue the pattern to work out the missing values.

4212	÷	54	=	78
4212	÷	5.4	=	780
4212	÷	0.54	=	....
4212	÷	0.054	=	....
4212	÷	0.0054	=	....

b Use the fact that 78 × 54 = 4212 to work out:

i 421.2 ÷ 54 = ...

ii 42.12 ÷ 5.4 = ...

iii 4.212 ÷ 0.54 = ...

3.8 Estimating and approximating

1 The mass of a baby is measured each month for seven months.

The results are shown in the table.

Month	0	1	2	3	4	5	6
Mass (kg)	3.4	4.5	5.7	6.5	7.1	7.6	8.0

a Work out the increase in mass each month. Complete the table.

Months	0–1	1–2	2–3	3–4	4–5	5–6
Increase in mass (kg)						

....

....

....

b Work out the mean increase in mass per month of the baby.

....

....

....

....

c Show how to check your answer using:

i estimation

....

....

....

ii inverse calculations

....

....

....

Mixed questions

1 Here are seven formula cards.

$$F = \frac{C}{0.1} + 5.02$$

$$H = 2F + G$$

$$E = 10 - 2B$$

$$C = E - G$$

$$G = 0.07 \times E$$

$$D = \frac{E}{4}$$

$$B = 0.01 \times A + 3$$

a Work out the value of H when $A = 27$.

Write down the order in which you used the cards.

....

....

....

....

....

....

....

....

....

....

....

....

b Which card do you NOT need to use work out H?

....

4 Length, mass and capacity

4.1 Choosing suitable units

1 Draw a line linking each description with its correct measurement and units.

The first one has been done for you.

The metric Olympics!

Distance of triathlon run	423 m
Mass of the men's javelin	50 m
Length of a swimming pool	600 g
Width of a swimming lane	40 km
Mass of the women's javelin	7.26 kg
Length of lane 4 on a running track	800 g
Length of a basketball court	10 km
Height of a high hurdle	4 kg
Distance of triathlon cycle	2.5 m
Mass of a shot in the men's shot put	1.5 km
Mass of a shot in the women's shot put	1.067 m
Distance of triathlon swim	28 m

Distance of triathlon run is linked to *10 km*.

2 The diagram shows a person standing next to a phone mast.

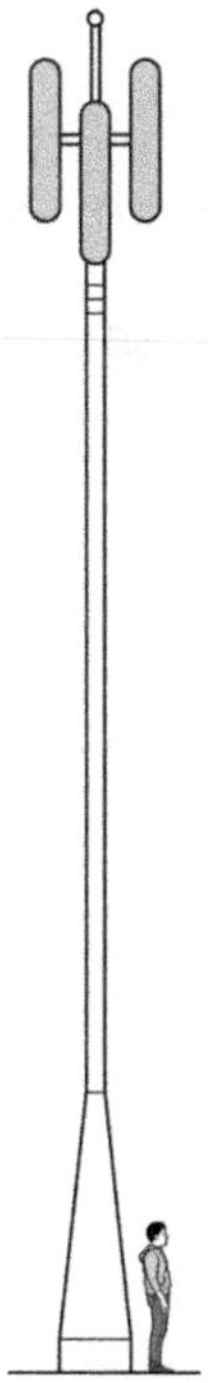

The tallest person in the world is 251 cm.

The shortest person in the world is 56 cm.

a What is the smallest height the phone mast could be?

....

....

b What is the difference between the biggest and smallest heights that the phone mast could be?

....

....

4.2 Kilometres and miles

1 Sofia is a delivery driver. She lives in Oxford.

On one day she must deliver parcels to London, Manchester and Birmingham.

She can deliver the parcels in any order, but she must start and finish in Oxford.

The table shows the distance between each of the cities in miles.

The sketch map shows the positions of the cities.

Distance between cities in miles

London			
60	Oxford		
125	75	Birmingham	
210	160	85	Manchester

Sketch map

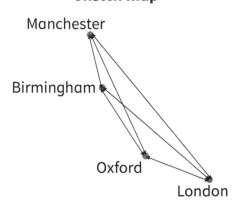

Work out the shortest route that Sofia can take. Give your answer in kilometres.

....

....

....

....

....

....

....

....

....

Mixed questions

1 Mia and Shen go on a two-day walk.

They draw graphs to show the distance they walk and their height above sea level each day.

Distance/height chart: Day 1

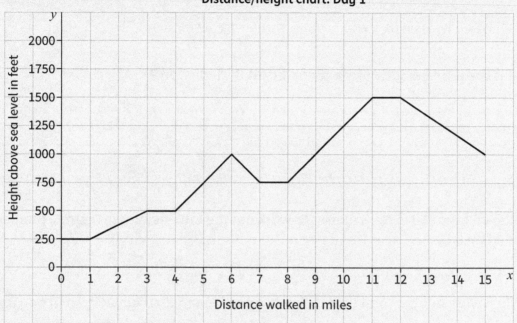

Distance walked in miles

Distance/height chart: Day 2

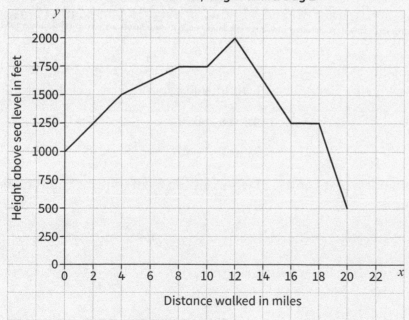

Distance walked in miles

a How many miles did they walk on:

i Day 1? .... **ii** Day 2? ....

b How many kilometres did they walk on:

i Day 1? .... **ii** Day 2? ....

c Complete the workings to find the total height, in feet, they CLIMBED UP on Day 1:

From 250 feet to 500 feet = 250 feet, from 500 feet to 1000 feet = 500 feet,

from 750 feet to 1500 feet = ... feet. Total = 250 + 500 + ... = ... feet

d What is the total height, in feet, they CLIMBED UP on Day 2?

....

....

....

e Use the fact that 10 feet ≈ 3 metres to work out the total height, in metres, they climbed up on:

i Day 1 .... **ii** Day 2 ....

Mia and Shen work out the total time it should take them to do their walk each day using this rule:

Total walk time = 1 hour for every 5 km walked + 1 hour for every 600 m height climbed up

f Complete these ratios:

1 hour : 5 km   1 hour : 600 m

...... minutes : 5 km   ...... minutes : 600 m

...... minutes : 1 km   ...... minutes : 10 m

g Use your answers from parts b), e) and f) to work out the total time it should take them to do their walk on:

i Day 1 ....

....

ii Day 2 ....

....

5.1 Parallel lines

1

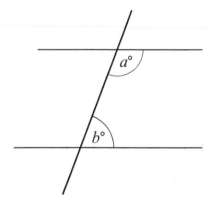

a and b are sometimes called **allied angles**.

Explain why allied angles add up to 180°. Use either corresponding angles or alternate angles in your explanation.

....

....

2

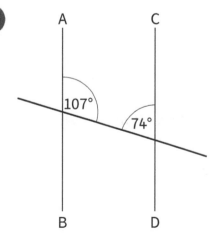

a   Are AB and CD parallel?

Circle the correct answer: YES   NO

Give a reason for your answer.

....

....

b   Will AB and CD meet if they are extended?

Circle the correct answer: YES   NO

If your answer is YES, work out the angle between them.

....

....

3 **a**

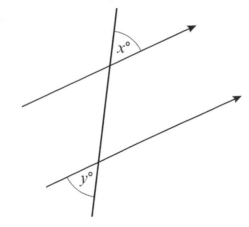

Explain why angles x and y must be equal.

....

....

b

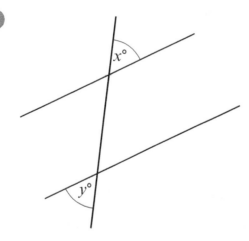

In this case the lines are NOT parallel (they are not drawn accurately) and angle x is bigger than angle y.

Do the extended lines meet on the left or on the right?

Circle the correct answer: LEFT   RIGHT

Give a reason for your answer.

....

....

5.2 Solving angle problems

This is a regular five-pointed star with rotational symmetry of order 5.

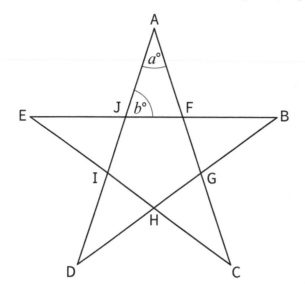

Angle FAJ = $a°$ and angle AJF = $b°$.

1 **a** Label any other angles that are equal to $a°$.

b Label any other angles that are equal to $b°$.

c Explain why $a + 2b = 180$.

....

....

d Use triangle ACI to explain why $b = 2a$.

....

....

e Use the results of parts c) and d) to work out a and b.

....

$a =$ .... $b =$ ....

f Find the size of each angle of the pentagon FGHIJ. Give a reason for your answer.

....

....

2 This pentagon has been divided into three triangles.

a What do the angles of each triangle add up to? ....

b Use this fact to explain why the sum of the angles of the pentagon must be 540°.

....

....

c

Show that the sum of the angles of this pentagon must be 540°.

....

....

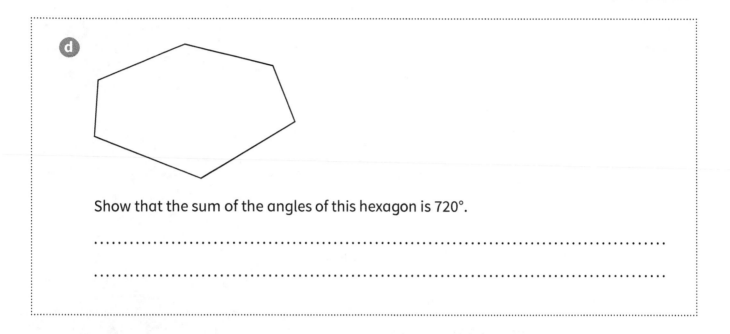

d

Show that the sum of the angles of this hexagon is 720°.

....

....

Mixed questions

1 One of the exterior angles of an isosceles triangle is 100°.

What are the angles of the triangle? | There are two possible answers. |

....

Draw sketches to illustrate your answers.

2

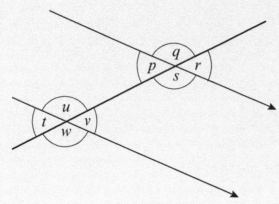

Insert a letter to make these statements correct.

a *p* and ...... are corresponding angles.

b *p* and ...... are angles on a straight line.

c *p* and ...... are allied angles.

d *p* and ...... are opposite angles.

e *p* and ...... are alternate angles.

f *p* and ...... are equal angles.

3 **a** Work out the mean of the three angles of any triangle.

....

b The mode of the angles of a triangle is 38°.

Find the other two angles.

....

c The range of the angles of a triangle is 30°.

Show that the smallest possible angle is 40° and the largest possible angle is 80°.

....

....

....

....

6.1 Collecting data

1 This section of a story contains 303 words.

'Look at that view; it is absolutely amazing!' said Lynn as they arrived at their lodge by the Zambezi river. 'Knew you'd like it,' replied Michelle with a grin. 'Now let's get unpacked and then we can head out for an evening drive to see what animals are around.' Quickly the six of them unpacked the two jeeps they had just driven from Harare. All the food and drink was put away in the kitchen, the luggage was put in the bedrooms and the cameras were unpacked ready for action. Lynn said, 'I cannot believe we are actually here in Zimbabwe with you all. And I cannot believe you are about to take us on our first ever game drive. I am so excited!' Carl replied 'Well, I am excited too, and I have been here loads of times! You and Greg come in the jeep with Michelle and me, and Nigel and Patch can follow in the second jeep. And no getting out of the jeep at all, as we do not want you to be eaten by a lion on day one! By the way, where are Nigel and Greg?' 'We are up here,' came a reply from upstairs. 'Lynn, come and have a look at this!' shouted Greg. 'I've counted twenty hippos in the water, and I can see three elephants on the bank on the opposite side of the river. Awesome!' Eventually they left to go on their game drive, cameras at the ready. They drove very slowly along the rutted tracks, keeping a lookout for signs of animal life. 'What is that over there, it looks like a dog with huge ears?' asked Lynn. 'Oh wow, Lynn, that is a painted dog,' replied Michelle. 'You are so lucky to see one of those as they are very rare!'

You are going to carry out a survey on the number of letters in the words in the story.

a Explain why you should have at least 30 words in your sample.

....

....

b Which of these options do you think is the best way to choose the words for your sample?

Explain your reasoning.

A The first 30 words in the story.

B The last 30 words in the story.

C 30 words from the middle of the story.

D The first word of the first 30 sentences.

E Every tenth word.

F Every other word until you have enough words.

G The first and last word of every line until you have enough words.

....

....

c Use the method you chose in part b) to get a sample of words from the story.

Underline the words that you are going to use.

d Complete these tally charts.

Number of letters in word	Tally	Frequency
1		
2		
3		
4		
5		
6		
7		
8		
9		
10+		
	Total	

Number of letters in word	Tally	Frequency
1–4		
5–8		
9–12		
	Total	

e Which of the tally charts in part d) is most useful in reaching a conclusion about the length of the words in the story? Explain your answer.

....

....

....

f Write a conclusion based on the data you have collected.

....

....

....

6.2 Types of data

1 Give an example of discrete data that some people may think is continuous data.

For example:

> I have asked 10 people their scores in a quiz. My results are 16, $16\frac{1}{2}$, 18, 19, $19\frac{1}{2}$, $10\frac{1}{2}$, 10, $17\frac{1}{2}$, 18, $14\frac{1}{2}$. This is continuous data as the values aren't whole numbers.

....

....

....

2 Give an example of continuous data that some people may think is discrete data.

For example:

> *I have asked 10 people their ages. My results are 23, 25, 22, 18, 36, 42, 12, 15, 17, 20. This is discrete data as the values are whole numbers.*

....

....

....

6.3 Using frequency tables

1 Here are some times, to the nearest minute, that 30 students took to complete a puzzle.

11	3	6	8	10	3	13	5	10	9
17	6	4	11	18	7	7	9	23	12
14	4	8	15	9	12	5	6	11	20

a Draw a grouped frequency table for this data.

Make sure your table has five or six class intervals and the intervals are the same size.

b Write a conclusion based on the results of your grouped frequency table.

....

....

....

....

2 80 students were asked their favourite English football team.

Of the 48 boys, $\frac{1}{4}$ chose Arsenal and $\frac{1}{3}$ chose Liverpool, but none chose Chelsea.

Of the girls, 25% chose Manchester City. This number is the same as the Chelsea total.

None of the girls chose Liverpool and only 1 chose Manchester United.

The total for Manchester United was 3 more than the total for Manchester City.

Complete the two-way table showing the information above.

	Arsenal	Chelsea	Liverpool	Manchester City	Manchester United	Total
Boys						
Girls						
Total						

....

....

....

....

Mixed questions

1 On safari, Greg takes 1500 photos of animals either eating, walking, running or playing.

$\frac{3}{10}$ of all the photos were of monkeys, and half of those were of monkeys playing, but none of them was of monkeys eating. The rest of the monkey photos were walking : running in the ratio 4 : 1.

There were the same number of photos of warthogs running as monkeys running. Of the 120 warthog photos, 30 were walking. The remainder of the warthog photos were of them eating.

$\frac{1}{2}$ of all the photos were of elephants. $\frac{2}{3}$ of the elephant photos were of them eating, 20% of them were walking. The rest of the elephant photos were of them playing.

The total number of photos of animals playing was 350.

There were 15 photos of impala walking. The ratio of the photos of impala eating : running was 5 : 2.

Complete the two-way table to show the information above.

	Eating	Walking	Running	Playing	Total
Elephant					
Monkey					
Impala					
Warthog					
Total					

....

....

....

7.1 Finding equivalent fractions, decimals and percentages

1 Write each fraction as **i** a decimal, **ii** a percentage.

a $\dfrac{8}{10}$ ....

b $\dfrac{9}{10}$ ....

c $\dfrac{10}{10}$ ....

d $\dfrac{11}{10}$ ....

e $\dfrac{12}{10}$ ....

f $\dfrac{18}{10}$ ....

2 Write each mixed number as **i** a decimal, **ii** a percentage.

a $1\dfrac{1}{4}$ ....

b $2\dfrac{27}{100}$ ....

c $3\dfrac{7}{50}$ ....

d $4\dfrac{4}{5}$ ....

7.2 Converting fractions to decimals

1 Write these numbers in order of size, starting with the smallest.

> Start by converting the fractions and percentages to decimals.

| 0.56 | $\dfrac{4}{7}$ | 0.6 | $\dfrac{7}{13}$ | 58.2% | $\dfrac{18}{27}$ | 55% | 0.5 |

....

....

....

....

7.3 Ordering fractions

1 The table shows Taos' scores in his end-of-year exams.

Subject	Score	Fraction	Equivalent fraction
Maths	61 out of 80		
English	11 out of 16		
Science	20 out of 32		
Thai	36 out of 48		
Business	27 out of 40		
History	14 out of 20		

In the table, write each score as a fraction, then write each score as an equivalent fraction using a common denominator for all the subjects.

List the subjects in order from the best score to the worst.

....

....

7.4 Adding and subtracting fractions

1 The diagram shows two statues. Each statue is made from three parts.

The height of each part, in metres, is shown.

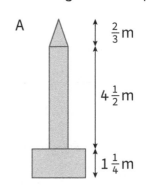

A

$\frac{2}{3}$ m

$4\frac{1}{2}$ m

$1\frac{1}{4}$ m

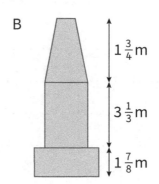

B

$1\frac{3}{4}$ m

$3\frac{1}{3}$ m

$1\frac{7}{8}$ m

a Which statue is the tallest? Show your working.

....

....

b What is the difference in the heights of the statues?

....

....

7.5 Finding fractions of a quantity

1 **a** Work out:

    i $\frac{1}{4}$ of \$40 and then $\frac{1}{2}$ of the answer.

    ....

    ii $\frac{1}{2}$ of \$40 and then $\frac{1}{4}$ of the answer

    ....

  b **i** What do you notice about your answers to a) i and ii?

    ....

    ii What is the overall fraction that you have found? How can you get this overall fraction from $\frac{1}{2}$ and $\frac{1}{4}$?

    ....

  c Work out:

    i $\frac{3}{5}$ of 60 kg and then $\frac{2}{3}$ of the answer.

    ....

    ii $\frac{2}{3}$ of 60 kg and then $\frac{3}{5}$ of the answer.

    ....

d **i** What do you notice about your answers to c) i and ii?

....

ii What is the overall fraction that you have found? How can you get this overall fraction from $\frac{3}{5}$ and $\frac{2}{3}$?

....

7.6 Multiplying an integer by a fraction

1 The cloud contains four fractions and the triangle contains four numbers.

$\frac{2}{3}$ $\frac{6}{7}$ $\frac{4}{5}$ $\frac{8}{11}$

385   420   462   480

a Choose a fraction from the cloud and a number from the triangle and multiply them together.

....

b When multiplied together, which fraction and number give you:

i the smallest possible answer? Work out this answer.

....

....

ii the largest possible answer? Work out this answer.

....

....

2 Work out the area of this rectangle.

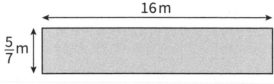

Give the answer as a mixed number.

....

....

7.7 Dividing an integer by a fraction

1 This rectangle has an area of 12 m².

$\frac{4}{5}$ m │ 12 m²

What is the length of the rectangle?

....

....

2 Sort these cards into four sets of correct calculations. There must be one oval, one rectangular and one star-shaped card in each set.

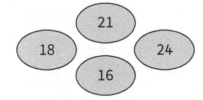

21   18   24   16

$\div \frac{3}{2}$ $\div \frac{7}{5}$ $= 12$ $= 14$

$\div \frac{6}{5}$ $\div \frac{8}{7}$ $= 15$ $= 20$

....

....

....

....

7.8 Multiplying and dividing fractions

1 The diagram shows a square joined to a rectangle.

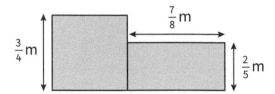

What is the total area of the shape?

....

....

2 The shaded area in this shape is $\frac{13}{30}$ m².

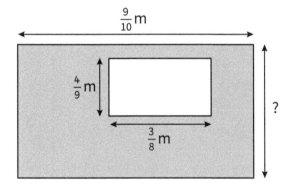

Work out the missing length.

....

....

....

....

Mixed questions

 1 Join the dominoes in the correct order from START to FINISH. Matching answers must be touching.

The first one is joined for you. One of the dominoes will be left over. Which one is it?

| $5\frac{14}{15} + 15\frac{2}{3}$ | $16 \times \frac{3}{7}$ | | $\frac{1}{2} + 1\frac{9}{14}$ | $18 \div \frac{5}{6}$ | | $2 \times \frac{4}{7}$ | $\frac{4}{9} \times \frac{15}{16}$ |

| $3\frac{14}{15} + 1\frac{2}{3}$ | $\frac{5}{2} \div \frac{7}{6}$ | | $9\frac{11}{21} - 2\frac{2}{3}$ | FINISH |

| START | $\frac{3}{8} \times \frac{5}{6}$ | $1\frac{1}{4} - \frac{15}{16}$ | $\frac{4}{5} \times 7$ |

8 Shapes and geometric reasoning

8.1 Recognising congruent shapes

1 Triangles ABC and CDE are congruent. ACD is a straight line.

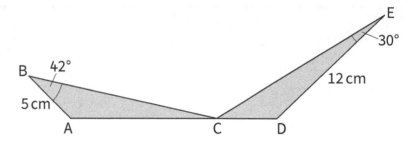

a Write down the length of AC ....

b Work out the length of AD ....

c Write down the size of: **i** ∠ BCA .... **ii** ∠ DCE ....

d Work out the size of ∠ BCE ....

....

2 In the diagram, the dotted line represents a line of symmetry.

ADE and CDG are straight lines.

∠ ABC = 115⁰, ∠ DGF = 70⁰ and ∠ BCD = 120⁰

Work out the value of ∠ CDE.

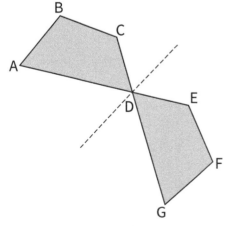

....

....

....

....

8.2 Identifying symmetry of 2D shapes

1 In the diagrams, the dotted lines are lines of symmetry. Complete each diagram.

a 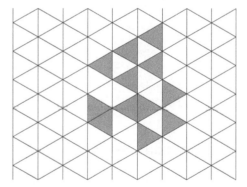 **b**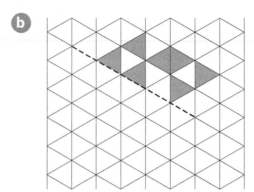

2 In this diagram, shade two more triangles so that the pattern has one line of symmetry.

Draw the line of symmetry on the diagram.

8.3 Classifying quadrilaterals

1 On the grid below, plot the following points:

(2, 2)   (6, 2)   (0, 4)   (4, 4)   (8, 4)   (2, 6)   (2, 8)   (6, 8)   (4, 9)

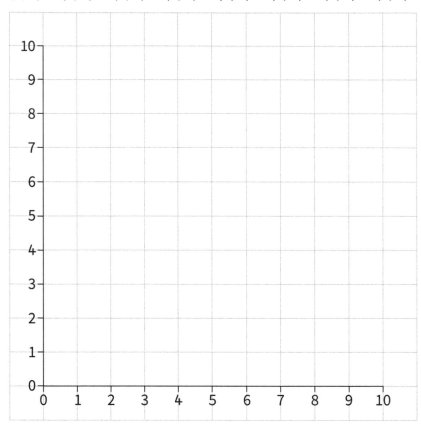

Which four points can you join to make each of these quadrilaterals?

a Rectangle ....

b Square ....

c Parallelogram ....

d Kite ....

e Trapezium ....

8.4 Drawing nets of solids

1 The diagram shows an L-shaped box.

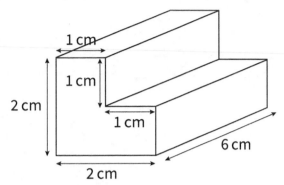

Draw a net for the box on the centimetre squar paper below.

2 The diagram shows a present and a sheet of wrapping paper.

Is there enough paper to wrap the present without cutting the paper? Explain your answer.

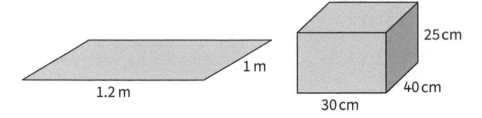

8.5 Making scale drawings

1 An office is 4.5 m long by 3 m wide. A scale drawing of the office is shown on the squared paper below.

Scale: 1 square represents 0.25 m

Add to the scale drawing of the office:

- a cupboard measuring 1.5 m long by 50 cm wide

- a desk measuring 1.75 m long by 0.75 m wide

- a chair for the desk measuring 75 cm by 75 cm

- two relaxing chairs measuring 75 cm by 75 cm

Arrange the items in the office in suitable positions and label each one.

Mixed questions

1 The diagram shows the pieces of a Tangram puzzle.

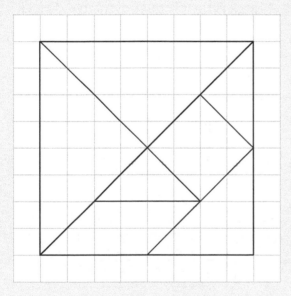

Copy the diagram on to squared paper and cut out all the pieces.

Work out how you can use all of the pieces to make each of these shapes.

a Rectangle

b Parallelogram

c Trapezium

d Triangle

e Hexagon

9.1 Collecting like terms

1 You simplify $2a \times 3a$ like this:

$2a \times 3a = 2 \times a \times 3 \times a = 2 \times 3 \times a \times a = 6a^2$

Simplify:

a $2a \times 5a =$ ....

b $3b \times 6b =$ ....

c $4c \times c =$ ....

2 Complete these multiplication pyramids. A brick is the product of the two bricks below it.

The first one has been started for you.

a

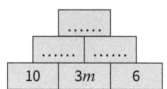

$4 \times 5 \longrightarrow$

b

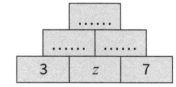

c

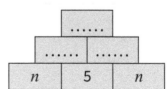

d

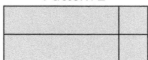

3 A pattern is made from rectangles and squares.

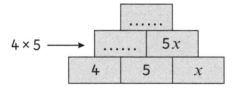

Pattern 1

Pattern 2

Pattern 3

a Write down and then simplify an algebraic expression for the area of:

i Pattern 1 ....

ii Pattern 2 ....

iii Pattern 3 ....

iv Pattern 4 ....

v Pattern 8 ....

b Write down and then simplify an algebraic expression for the perimeter of:

i Pattern 1 ....

ii Pattern 2 ....

iii Pattern 3 ....

iv Pattern 4 ....

v Pattern 8 ....

9.2 Expanding brackets

1 Write down and then simplify an expression for the area of each of these rectangles.

a $(2x + 1)$ cm

4 cm

....

....

b $(3y - 2)$ cm

$2y$ cm

....

....

2 Write down and then simplify an expression for the area of this compound shape.

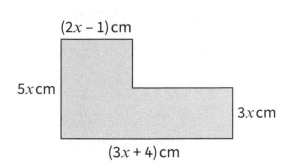

$(2x - 1)$ cm

$5x$ cm

$3x$ cm

$(3x + 4)$ cm

3 Fill in the missing numbers and letters in these expressions.

Use all the numbers and letters from the cloud.

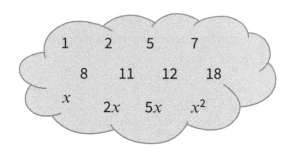

1   2   5   7

8   11   12   18

x

$2x$ $5x$ x^2

a $4(3x + \ldots) = \ldots x + 28$

b $3x(2x - \ldots) = 6\ldots - 3x$

c $6(\ldots - 3) = 30x - \ldots$

d $\ldots x(9 - \ldots) = 45x - 5x^2$

e $2(\ldots x + 4) + 3(4x - \ldots) = 16x - 16$

f $x(4x + 1) - \ldots(x - 5) = 2x^2 + \ldots x$

9.3 Constructing and solving equations

1 A square has a side length of x cm.

A rectangle has a length of $x + 2$ cm and a width of 2 cm.

The square has the same perimeter as the rectangle.

Work out the value of x.

....

....

....

....

2 The total area of this rectangle is 52 cm².

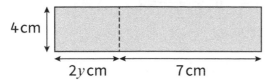

4 cm

2*y* cm   7 cm

Work out the value of *y*.

....

....

....

....

3 Amy and Ben live on the same floor in a block of flats.

They meet on the ground floor and Amy starts up the stairs when Ben presses the button for the lift.

Amy takes 18 seconds to go up one floor using the stairs.

a Write an expression for the time it takes her to go up *x* floors. ....

Ben waits 40 seconds for the lift. It then takes him 8 seconds per floor to go up in the lift.

b Write an expression for the time it takes him to go up *x* floors. ....

They both arrive at their floor at the same time.

c Which floor do they live on? ....

4 **a** Complete the workings to solve this equation.

$$\frac{x + 4}{6} = 3 \qquad x + 4 = 3 \times 6$$

$$x + 4 = 18$$

....

....

b Solve the following.

i $\dfrac{x+2}{7} = -4$

....

....

....

....

ii $\dfrac{3x-1}{2} = 7$

....

....

....

....

Mixed questions

1 Here is a secret code box.

8	11	8	3	7	4	5	2	9

Solve each equation below.

Use your answers to fill in the letters into the code box to find the name of a Winter Olympic sport.

L	$4(x-5) = 8$
H	$2(x+3) = 3x - 3$
O	$\dfrac{x-5}{6} = 1$
I	$5x + 3 - 2x - 1 = 17$

G	$2(2x+3) + 5x = 24$
E	$12 + 3(x+4) = 36$
S	$30 = 6(2x-1)$
B	$2(x-5) = 3(2x-14)$

....

....

....

....

10 Processing and presenting data

10.1 Calculating statistics from discrete data

Mia wants to find the mean of these five lengths, in centimetres.

125   118   122   130   111

She starts by subtracting 120 from every number.

5   −2   2   10   −9

She finds the mean of these five numbers.
$$\frac{5 + -2 + 2 + 10 + -9}{5} = \frac{6}{5} = 1.2$$
She adds this to 120.

The mean is 121.2.

This method of working out the mean makes the arithmetic easier, so you do not need a calculator.

You do not have to subtract 120. You can choose any convenient number.

---

1 Check that Mia's method gives the correct answer.

....

Use Mia's method to find the mean in the following questions.

2 Find the mean of these masses.   Start by subtracting 50 kg.

53 kg   48 kg   55 kg   50 kg   49 kg

....

....

3 Find the mean of these ages.   Start by subtracting 40.

35   36   39   40   40   42   48   50

....

....

4 Find the mean of these times, in minutes.

75   80   70   69   74   79   76   66   73   70

....

....

5 Find the mean of these lengths, in millimetres.

440   440   440   445   445   450   450   450   455   460   460   465

....

....

6 Here are six numbers.

4   4   5   6   10   13

The mean of these numbers is 7.

Use this fact to write down the mean of each of these sets of numbers.

a 24, 24, 25, 26, 30, 33   mean = ...

b 114, 114, 115, 116, 120, 123   mean = ...

c 16, 16, 17, 18, 22, 25   mean = ...

d 8, 8, 10, 12, 20, 26   mean = ...

e 40, 40, 50, 60, 100, 130   mean = ...

You can also use Mia's method in a frequency table.

Here are the ages of 40 people.

Age	25	26	27	28	29
Frequency	5	8	14	10	3

Here is Mia's way to work out the mean ages.

Take 27 from the ages to work out the mean.

Age − 27 = a	−2	−1	0	1	2	Total
Frequency f	5	8	14	10	3	40
$a \times f$	−10	−8	0	10	6	−2

Mean $= \dfrac{-2}{40} = -0.5$

Add on the mean age = 27 − 0.5 = 26.95

Use Mia's method to find the mean from these frequency tables. Use the extra rows in the tables to do this.

7

Mass (kg)	45	46	47	48	49	Total
Frequency	8	6	11	15	10	50

....

.... Mean = ... kg

8

Height (cm)	72	73	74	75	76	77	Total
Frequency	10	25	33	20	4	8	100

....

.... Mean = ... cm

10.2 Using statistics

1 This bar chart shows the masses of 150 people.

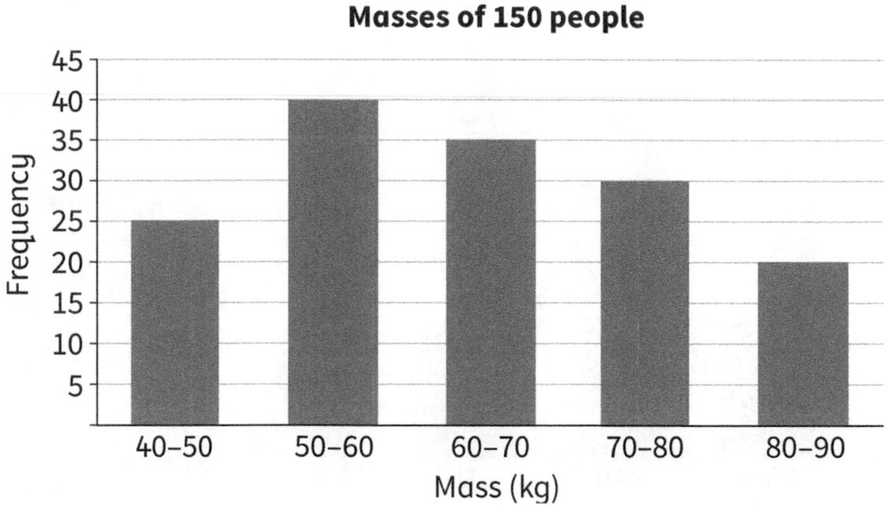

Masses of 150 people

a Estimate the mean mass.

Mean = ... kg

b Here are three statements. Tick (✓) the one that is correct.

The mean is larger than the median . . . .

The mean is smaller than the mode . . . .

You cannot tell which is larger . . . .

Give a reason for your answer.

. . . .

. . . .

2 This bar chart shows the heights of 40 boys and 25 girls.

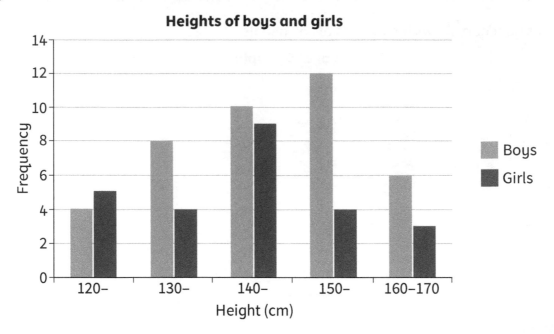

Complete the sentence below. Insert a number and delete the word 'more' or 'less'.

The mean height of the girls is . . . . cm more/less than the mean height of the boys.

Put your working in the space below.

Mixed questions

1 The mean mass of 20 men is 63.5 kg.

The mean mass of 15 women is 53.2 kg.

Calculate the mean mass of all 35 people.

....

....

.... Mean = ... kg

2 This table shows the heights of 40 tomato plants.

Height (cm)	20–24	25–29	30–34	35–40
Frequency	5	8	20	7

a Estimate the mean height of the 40 plants.

.... cm

b Explain why the smallest possible value for the actual mean height is 28.625 cm.

....

....

....

3 This table shows the number of characters in 50 internet passwords.

Characters	8	9	10	11	12
Frequency	4	20			9

Two of the frequencies are missing.

What can you say about the mean number of characters of the 50 passwords?

....

....

....

11 Percentages

11.1 Calculating percentages

1 Work out:

a 15% of $60 = ...

b 60% of $15 = ...

c 85% of $30 = ...

d 30% of $85 = ...

e 22% of 90 kg = ...

f 90% of 22 kg = ...

2 **a** What do you notice about the answers to Question 1?

....

b Write down a generalisation based on your answer to part a).

....

Percentages can be bigger than 100%.

For example, what is 160% of 7000 people?

160% as a decimal is 1.6.

160% of 7000 is 1.6 × 7000 = 11 800

3 Work out:

a 180% of 30 kg = ...

b 240% of 40 minutes = ...

c 145% of $450 = ...

d 350% of 800 people = ...

e 105% of $350 = ...

f 350% of $105 = ...

It is not always possible to have a percentage bigger than 100.

4 This week 240 people went to the cinema.

a Maha says: 'Last week there were 150% more.'

Show that there were 600 people last week.

....

b Anders says: 'Last week there were 150% less.'

Explain why this is impossible.

....

5 Are these statements possible or impossible? Circle the correct answer.

a My income is 150% of yours.   POSSIBLE   IMPOSSIBLE

b I had a pay rise of 110%.   POSSIBLE   IMPOSSIBLE

c I gave my brother 125% of my money.   POSSIBLE   IMPOSSIBLE

d The population of the city went up by 135%.   POSSIBLE   IMPOSSIBLE

e The population of the city went down by 103%.   POSSIBLE   IMPOSSIBLE

f 120% of the people voted for the president.   POSSIBLE   IMPOSSIBLE

6 Complete this table.

75%	100%	125%	175%	225%	275%
	$36				

7 Complete this table.

25%	100%	150%	175%	190%	210%
		480 kg			

11.2 Percentage increases and decreases

The price of a television is $460. The price increases by 4%.

Here is a quick way to calculate the new price:

$450 is 100%.

The new price is 100% + 4% = 104%

104% of $460 is 1.04 × 460 = $478.40.

Use the same method to answer the following questions.

1. The price of a guitar is $320. The price increases by 7%.

   Find the new price.

   .... $ . . . .

2. Twenty years ago the population of a town was 65 000.

   The population now is 26% higher.

   Find the population now.

   ....

3. Jake earns $840 a week. He gets a pay rise of 14%.

   Work out how much he earns each week now.

   .... $ . . . .

4. The height of a tree five years ago was 2.60 m. Now it is 65% taller.

   Work out the height now.

   .... m

You can use the same method for percentage decreases.

The price of a car is $12 600.

The price is reduced by 6%.

100% − 6% = 94%

The reduced price is 0.94 × 12 600 = $11 844.

5 The price of a coat is $135.

In a sale the price is reduced by 30%.

Calculate the sale price.

.... $ ....

6 The mass of a man is 72.5 kg.

He goes on a diet and reduces his mass by 8%.

Calculate his new mass.

....kg

7 The population of a town 50 years ago was 128 000.

Now the population has reduced by 55%.

Calculate the population now.

....

8 The price of a computer is $450.

The price is increased by 15%.

A month later the price is reduced by 15%.

Razi says: 'The price now is $450 again.'

Show why Razi is not correct.

....

....

Mixed questions

1 Look at these sale signs.

Shoes	Coat
Normal price $85.00	Normal price $140.00
Sale price $72.25	Sale price ....

The price of the coat is reduced by the same percentage as the price of the shoes.

Calculate the sale price of the coat.

....

....

....

2 In the middle of 2016, the world population was 7.40 billion.

The population is increasing by 3.4% every ten years.

a If the rate of increase does not change, show that the population in 2026 will be 7.65 billion.

....

b Complete this table to show the population in future years if the rate of increase stays the same.

Year	2016	2026	2036	2046	2056
Population (billions)	7.40	7.65			

3 The price of a refrigerator is $420.

a The price is reduced in a sale by 20%.

Calculate the sale price.

.... $ ....

b Later the price is reduced again, this time by 10%.

Calculate the new price.

.... $ ....

c Calculate the overall percentage reduction, after the two decreases.   It is not 30%!

....

....%

4 The rent of an apartment in 2014 was $640 a month.

In 2015 the rent increased by 10%.

In 2016 the rent increased by 10% again.

Calculate the rent in 2016.

.... $ ....

Calculate the overall percentage increase from 2014 to 2016.

....

....%

12 Constructions

12.1 Drawing circles and arcs

1 Without looking at the Coursebook, label the parts of the circle. Use all the words from the box below.

> sector   circumference   arc   diameter   radius   centre   chord   segment

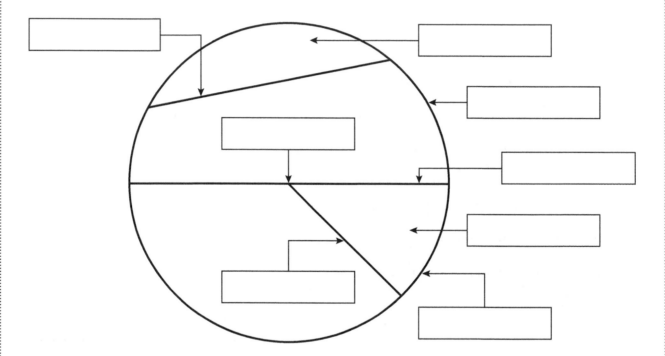

2 Make accurate copies of these diagrams.

a

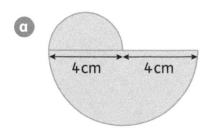

4 cm   4 cm

b

5 cm   5 cm

c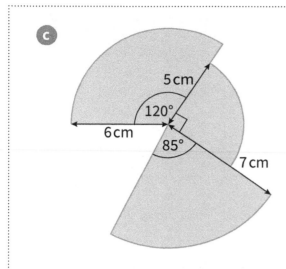

12.2 Drawing a perpendicular bisector

1 The diagram shows a drawing of a field, ABCD.

Divide the field into four sections by drawing the perpendicular bisectors of AB and AD.

A farmer wants to plant maize in the largest section and peas in the smallest section of the field.

He wants to grow more potatoes than carrots.

Label each section of the field with the crop that the farmer will plant.

2 **a** Make an accurate drawing of this rhombus.

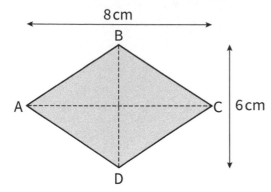

8 cm

6 cm

Start by drawing the line AC, then draw the perpendicular bisector.

b Measure and write down the length of the side of the rhombus. . . . .

3 The diagram shows triangle EFG.

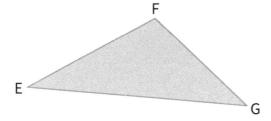

a Draw the perpendicular bisectors for the lines:

i EF   **ii** FG   **iii** EG

Mark a dot where all three bisectors cross and label it O.

b **i** Using compasses, draw a circle with centre O and radius EO.

ii What do you notice about all three vertices of the triangle and the circle?

. . . .

12.3 Drawing an angle bisector

1   The diagram shows triangle HIJ.

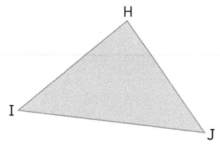

a   Draw the angle bisectors for:

   i   ∠HIJ   **ii**   ∠HJI   **iii**   ∠IHJ

Mark a dot where all three bisectors cross and label it O.

b   **i**   Using compasses, draw the largest circle you can with centre O that does not go outside the triangle.

   ii   What do you notice about the sides of the triangle and the circle?

....

2   The diagram shows a reflex angle of 320°.

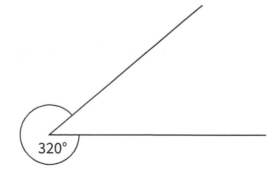

320°

a   Use compasses to bisect the following angles:

   i   The 320° angle   **ii**   One of the 160° angles

   iii One of the 80° angles   **iv**   One of the 40° angles

b   Use a protractor to check the accuracy of your 20° angle.

12.4 Constructing triangles

1 Without using a protractor, draw an equilateral triangle with side length 6 cm.

2 A farmer has a triangular field with sides of length 180 m, 150 m and 95 m.

In your notebook, draw an accurate scale drawing of the field using a scale of 1 cm represents 20 m.

Mixed questions

1 The diagram shows line AC. B is the centre of the line. $\angle$ ABC = 180°.

Using only compasses, construct an angle of 135° at B.

90° + 45° = 135°

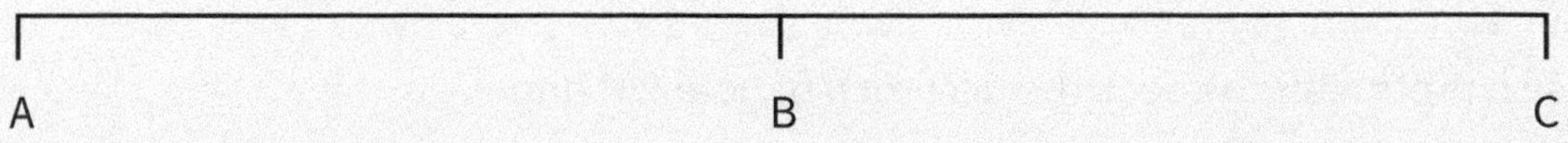

A   B   C

13 Graphs

13.1 Equations of the form $y = mx + c$

1 The equation of a straight line is not always in the form $y = mx + c$.

For example, the equation of a straight line could be $x + y = 2$.

This means that the coordinates of any point on the line add up to 2.

a Complete this table of pairs of numbers that add up to 2.

x	5	4	2	1	−1	−2
y	−3		0		3	

b Three points are marked on this grid.

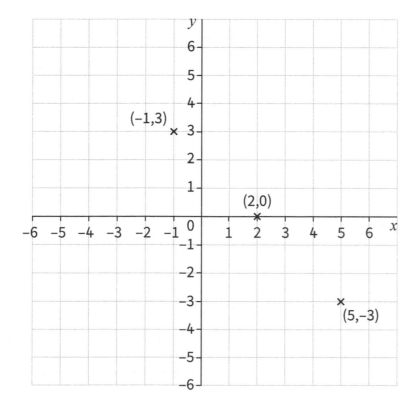

Plot the rest and draw a straight line through them.

2 The equation of a straight line is $x + y = 4$.

This means that the coordinates of any point on the line add up to 4.

a Complete this table of pairs of numbers that add up to 4.

x	5	4	2	0	−1	−2
y		0			5	

b Mark the points on this grid and draw a straight line through them.

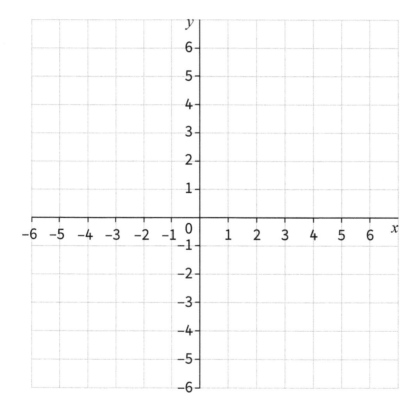

c If the grid is extended, is (11, −7) on the line? Give a reason for your answer.

....

....

3 The equation of a line is $x + y = 0$.

a Explain why the points (2, –2) and (–5, 5) must be on this line.

....

....

b Draw the line on this grid.

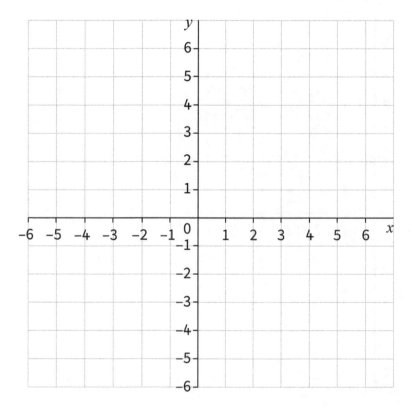

c If the grid is extended, explain why (12, –10) is above the line.

....

....

4 The equation of a straight line is $x + 2y = 0$.

One point on the line is $(4, -2)$ because $4 + 2 \times -2 = 0$.

a Complete this table of points.

x	6	4	2	0	−2	−4
y		−2			1	

b Draw the line on this grid and label it.

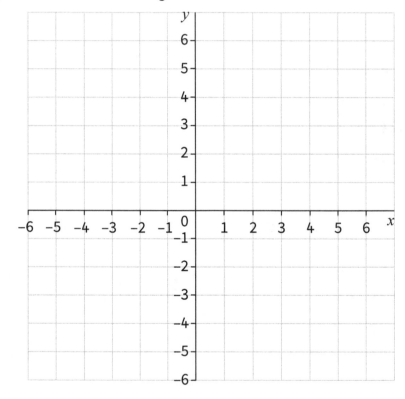

c The equation of another line is $2x + y = 0$.

Explain why $(-3, 6)$ must be on this line.

....

....

d Complete this table of points on the line $2x + y = 0$.

x	−3	−2	−1	0	1	2
y	6					−4

e Draw and label the line $2x + y = 0$ on the grid in part b).

5 Here are equations of lines written in two different ways.

Match the equations. One has been done for you.

$x + y = 4$ ——————— $y = -x + 4$

$x + y = 2$ $\qquad\qquad\qquad$ $y = -2x$

$x + y = 0$ $\qquad\qquad\qquad$ $y = -\dfrac{1}{2}x$

$x + 2y = 0$ $\qquad\qquad\qquad$ $y = -x$

$2x + y = 0$ $\qquad\qquad\qquad$ $y = -x + 2$

13.2 The midpoint of a line segment

1 Draw a line to match each pair of points to the correct midpoint.

$(4, 0)$ and $(0, -4)$

$\qquad\qquad\qquad\qquad$ $(-2, 2)$

$(-3, 6)$ and $(-1, -2)$

$\qquad\qquad\qquad\qquad$ $(2, -2)$

$(-5, 1)$ and $(1, -5)$

$\qquad\qquad\qquad\qquad$ $(2, 2)$

$(-6, 2)$ and $(10, -6)$

$\qquad\qquad\qquad\qquad$ $(-2, -2)$

$(-1, -1)$ and $(-3, 5)$

2

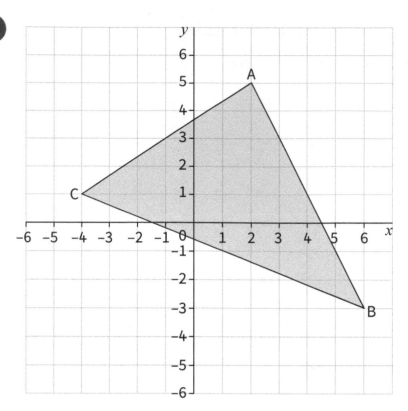

a Work out the coordinates of these points and mark them on the grid.

D, the midpoint of BC

.... D (...... , ...)

E, the midpoint of AC

.... E (...... , ...)

F, the midpoint of AB

.... F (...... , ...)

b Show that the midpoint of EF is also the midpoint of AD.

....

....

3 The midpoint of a line segment is (–4, 5).

One end of the line segment is (1, –1).

Work out the coordinates of the other end of the line segment.

....

....

4 The midpoint of a line segment is (0, 0).

What can you say about the coordinates of the end points of the line segment?

....

....

Mixed questions

1 Draw these lines on the graph below.

a $y = 2x + 2$ **b** $y = 2x - 2$ **c** $y + 2x = 2$

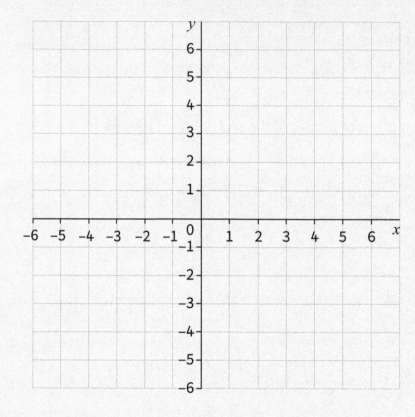

....

....

....

....

2 The vertices of a square are $(-2, 2)$, $(3, 4)$, $(5, -1)$ and $(0, -3)$.

Find the coordinates of the centre of the square.

....

....

3 Look at the lines on this grid.

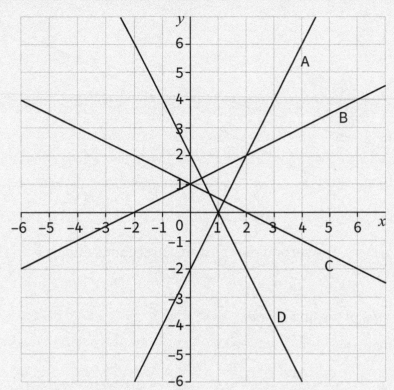

Match each equation to one of the lines on the graph. Write the line letter next to the equation.

$y = \dfrac{1}{2}x + 1$ ......

$y + \dfrac{1}{2}x = 1$ ......

$x = \dfrac{1}{2}y + 1$ ......

$x + \dfrac{1}{2}y = 1$ ......

4

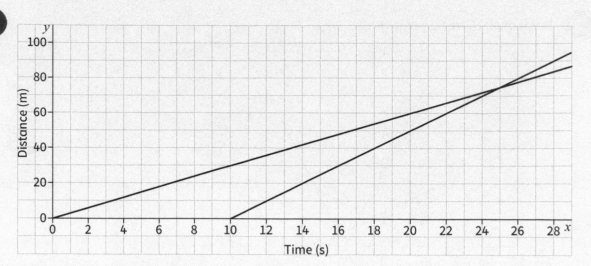

The graph shows two runners. The second runner starts 10 seconds after the first runner.

a Work out the speed, in m/s, of the first runner.

....

b Work out the speed, in m/s, of the second runner.

....

c Work out how long it takes for the second runner to catch the first runner.

....

d Insert a number to complete this equation for the line representing the first runner.

$y = \ldots\ldots x$

e Insert two numbers to complete this equation for the line representing the second runner.

$y = \ldots\ldots x + \ldots\ldots$

14 Ratio and proportion

14.1 **Simplifying ratios**

Fractions can be written as a ratio and simplified in the following way.

First rewrite the fractions with a common denominator: $\frac{1}{2}:\frac{1}{3}=\frac{3}{6}:\frac{2}{6}$

Both fractions can then be multiplied by 6, giving the ratio $3:2$.

---

1 Write each ratio in its simplest form.

> The fractions in part a) already have a common denominator.

a $\frac{1}{4}:\frac{3}{4}$ **b** $\frac{1}{4}:\frac{1}{8}$ **c** $\frac{2}{3}:\frac{3}{5}$

....

....

2 Write each ratio in its simplest form. The first one has been done for you.

a $20\%:80\%$ **b** $30\%:60\%$ **c** $25\%:15\%$ **d** $63\%:39\%$

   $20:80$ ....

    $1:4$ ....

3 Maria plants flowers in her garden. $\frac{2}{5}$ of her flowers are tulips, the rest are daffodils.

Write the ratio of tulips : daffodils in its simplest form.

....

4 In a class of students, 85% are right-handed and the rest are left-handed.

Write down the ratio of right-handed : left-handed students in its simplest form.

....

5 Any ratio can be written in the form $1:n$ or $n:1$ like this:

In the form $1:n$,   ÷4 ⌒ 4:10 ⌒ ÷4   1:2.5

In the form $n:1$,   ÷10 ⌒ 4:10 ⌒ ÷10   0.4:1

Write these ratios in the form **i** $1:n$ and **ii** $n:1$

a   **i** 2:4   **ii** 2:4   **b**   **i** 4:15   **ii** 4:15

....

....

c   **i** 0.3:0.9   **ii** 0.3:0.9   **d**   **i** 25:165   **ii** 25:165

....

....

14.2 Sharing in a ratio

1 Salim draws a quadrilateral. The angles are in the ratio $1:4:5:2$.

Calculate the largest angle in the quadrilateral.

....

....

2 There are 24 coins in Angela's purse.

The ratio of 50 cent to 25 cent to 10 cent coins is $2:3:7$.

a How many 10 cent coins does she have?

....

....

b How much money does she have in her purse in total?

....

....

3 Heidi makes her favourite colour paint by mixing blue, yellow and green in the ratio 0.8 : 1.1 : 0.1.

Complete the table to show how much of each colour she needs to make the quantities shown.

Size of tin	Blue	Yellow	Green
1 litre			
1.5 litres			
2.5 litres			

....

....

....

....

4 Tips in a restaurant are shared between the waiters, chefs and kitchen help in the ratio 4 : 5 : 1.

On Saturday the total tips were $425.35.

On Wednesday the total tips were $146.23.

How much more did the waiters get on Wednesday than the kitchen help on Saturday?

....

....

....

....

....

14.3 **Solving problems**

1 A recipe to serve eight people uses the following ingredients.

400 g rice
2.4 litres stock
1 kg fish
480 g mixed vegetables

How much of each ingredient do you need to serve three people?

....

....

....

....

2 Aliash makes a drink using squash and water in the ratio 5 : 27.

Bivna makes a drink using squash and water in the ratio 3 : 16.

a Write each ratio in the form 1 : n.

....

b Whose drink is stronger? Explain why.

....

3 A shopkeeper has two offers on health bars.

Offer 1
5 health bars
$1.80

Offer 2
3 health bars
$......

The shop keeper decides to charge $1\frac{1}{2}$ times as much per bar on Offer 2 than on Offer 1.

What is the missing price on Offer 2?

....

....

Mixed questions

1 **a** On a piece of paper, draw three squares with side lengths of 3 cm, 4 cm and 5 cm.

Measure the length of the diagonal of each square.

Complete the table below.

Length of side	Length of diagonal	Ratio of lengths side : diagonal	Ratio of lengths side : diagonal in the form 1 : n
3 cm			
4 cm			
5 cm			

b What do you notice about the ratios in the form 1 : n?

....

....

c What do you think the length of the diagonal will be for a square with side length 8 cm?

....

d What do you think the length of the diagonal will be for a square with side length 14.14 cm?

....

2 All three of these photographs have their sides in the same ratio.

A
12 cm

8 cm

B
? cm

16 cm

C
36 cm

? cm

a Work out the missing lengths in pictures B and C.

....

....

b Write down the ratio, in its simplest form, of the side lengths of the pictures.

i A : B .... **ii** A : C ....

c Work out the area of each picture.

....

....

d Write down the ratio, in its simplest form, of the areas of the pictures.

i A : B .... **ii** A : C ....

e What do you notice about your answers to parts b) and d)?

....

....

15 Probability

15.1 Equally likely outcomes

1

| 1 | 2 | 3 | 4 | 5 | 6 | 7 | 8 | 9 | 10 |

Alicia has ten cards numbered 1 to 10.

She takes cards one at a time, at random.

a The first card is even.

Find the probability that the second card is even.

....

b The first two cards are even.

Find the probability that the third card is even.

....

c The first four cards are odd.

Find the probability that the fifth card is odd.

....

2 **a** Ahmed has two different pairs of socks in a drawer.

He takes out one sock at random. Then he takes a second sock.

Find the probability that he has taken a pair of socks.

....

b Ahmed has three different pairs of socks in a drawer.

What is the answer to part a) in this case?

....

c Ahmed has ten different pairs of socks in a drawer.

What is the answer to part a) in this case?

....

3 A computer generates at random four digits that are either 0 or 1.

An example is 0110.

a Find the probability that the first digit is 0. ....

b Find the probability that the first two digits are 0. ....

c Find the probability that all four digits are 0. ....

4 Xavier has some cards with numbers on.

He takes a card at random.

The probability that the card is a multiple of 3 is $\frac{1}{2}$.

The probability the card is a multiple of 5 is $\frac{1}{3}$.

What is the smallest possible number of cards Xavier has?

....

....

15.2 Listing all possible outcomes

1 On a menu there are two drinks and three sandwiches.

Drink	Sandwich
Juice	Cheese
Coffee	Tuna
	Egg

a List all the possible choices of a drink and a sandwich.

....

....

b The most likely choice of a drink and a sandwich is coffee and cheese.

This has a probability of $\frac{1}{2}$.

All the other choices are equally likely.

Work out the probability that someone chooses juice and egg.

....

c There are three types of dessert on the menu.

Drink	Sandwich	Dessert
Juice	Cheese	Fruit
Coffee	Tuna	Yogurt
	Egg	Cake

How many different ways are there of choosing a drink, a sandwich and a dessert?

....

....

2 A red dice and a blue dice are thrown at the same time.

Find the probability of the following.

a Throwing a total of 6.

....

b Throwing a product of 6.

....

c The number on the red dice being greater than the number on the blue dice.

....

d Both dice showing a prime number.

....

3 Jake and Mia are in a room with three other students.

The teacher chooses two students at random.

Find the probability that the teacher chooses:

a both Jake and Mia.

....

b one of Jake and Mia but not both.

....

Mixed questions

1 In a game a light can be red, blue, green or yellow.

The probability it is red is 0.15.

The probability it is red or blue is 0.25.

The probability it is red or blue or yellow is 0.65.

Fill in this table of probabilities.

Colour	Red	Blue	Green	Yellow
Probability				

2 A spinner has 24 equal sectors, coloured red, white or blue.

The probability that the spinner shows white is $\frac{1}{3}$.

The probability that the spinner shows blue is $\frac{1}{4}$.

How many sectors are red?

....

3 There are red, blue and black pens in a box.

A student takes a pen at random.

The probability that the pen is not red is $\frac{3}{4}$.

The probability that the pen is not blue is $\frac{2}{3}$.

Find the probability that the pen is not black.

....

....

4 50 students each spin a coin until it lands on a head.

Each student records the number of throws it took. The results are shown in the table below.

Throws	1	2	3	4	5	6	7
Frequency	22	15	5	5	2	0	1

Use the data to find the experimental probabilities of these outcomes:

a Exactly three throws to get a head.

....

b Getting a head in less than four throws.

....

c Needing more than two throws to get a head.

....

5 There are six girls and four boys in a room.

Each boy is the brother of one of the girls.

The teacher chooses a girl at random and a boy at random.

Find the probability that the teacher chooses a brother and sister.

....

....

16.1 Transforming shapes

1 The diagram shows two triangles, A and B.

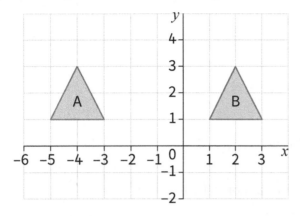

Describe the reflection that takes triangle A to triangle B.

....

2 The diagram shows two triangles, C and D.

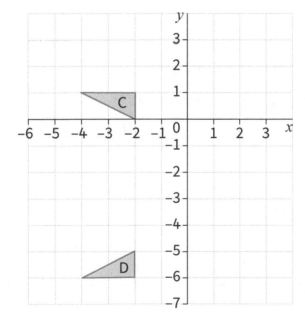

Describe the reflection that takes triangle C to triangle D.

....

3 The diagram shows triangles ABC and DEF.

Triangle ABC has been reflected to make DEF.

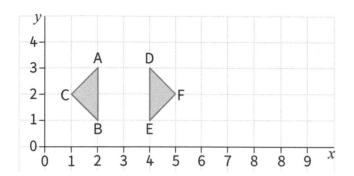

a Write down the equation of the mirror line. ....

b Triangle DEF is reflected in the line $x = 6$ to become triangle GHI.

Complete the table showing the coordinates of the three vertices of the triangles.

Triangle ABC	A (2, 3)	B (2, 1)	C (1, 2)
Triangle DEF	D (4, 3)	E (......, ...)	F (......, ...)
Triangle GHI	G (......, ...)	H (......, ...)	I (......, ...)

c Triangle GHI is reflected in the line $x = 9$ to become triangle JKL.

Triangle JKL is reflected in the line $x = 12$ to become triangle MNP.

Without drawing the triangles, use your answers to part b) to help you work out the coordinates of triangles JKL and MNP.

Complete the table below.

Triangle JKL	J (......, ...)	K (......, ...)	L (......, ...)
Triangle MNP	M (......, ...)	N (......, ...)	P (......, ...)

Explain how you worked out your answers.

....

....

16.2 Enlarging shapes

1 The diagram shows three rectangles, P, Q and R, drawn on centimetre square paper.

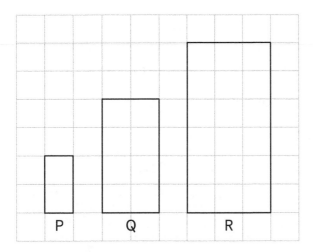

a Write down the scale factor of the enlargement of the following rectangles.

i P to Q . . . .

ii P to R . . . .

iii Q to R . . . .

b Complete the tables below.

Rectangle	Perimeter (cm)	Area (cm²)
P		
Q		
R		

Rectangles	Ratio of lengths	Ratio of perimeters	Ratio of areas
P : Q	1 : 2	1 :	1 : . . . . . .
P : R	1 :	1 :	1 : . . . . . .
Q : R	2 :	. . . . . :	. . . . . : . . . . . .

c What do you notice about the ratios you found in part b)?

....

....

....

d Jake draws a shape that has a perimeter of 8 cm and an area of 3 cm².

He enlarges the shape using a scale factor of 4. Work out:

i the perimeter of the enlarged shape

....

ii the area of the enlarged shape

....

Mixed questions

1 The diagram shows a shape on a grid.

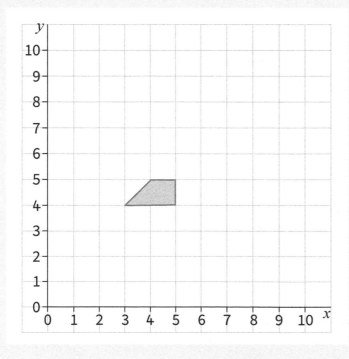

(a) Draw the image of the shape after a rotation of 90° anticlockwise about the point (5, 5).

Rotate the new image 90° anticlockwise about the point (5, 5), and repeat the same rotation again.

(b) What is the order of rotation of the combined final shape? ....

(c) Add to your diagram an enlargement of the combined final shape by a scale factor of 2, centre (5, 5).

2 Harsha makes these triangular cards.

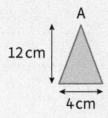

A

12 cm

4 cm

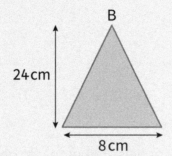

B

24 cm

8 cm

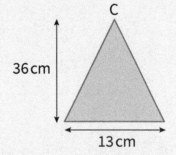

C

36 cm

13 cm

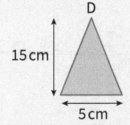

D

15 cm

5 cm

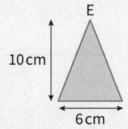

E

10 cm

6 cm

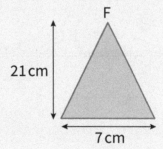

F

21 cm

7 cm

Which of the cards are not enlargements of the smallest card? Explain your answer.

....

....

....

17 Area, perimeter and volume

17.1 The area of a triangle

1 Work out the missing measurements for each triangle.

a
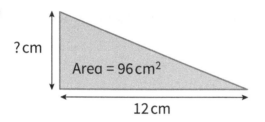

? cm

Area = 96 cm²

12 cm

....

....

....

b
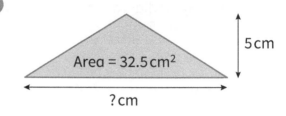

5 cm

Area = 32.5 cm²

? cm

....

....

....

2 Work out the area of these triangles. Remember to give the units with your answers.

a
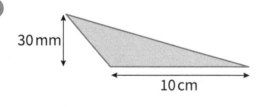

30 mm

10 cm

....

....

....

b
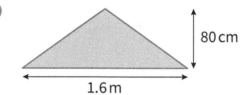

80 cm

1.6 m

....

....

....

3 Write down the base length and height of five triangles that have an area of 12 cm².

....

....

....

17.2 The areas of a parallelogram and trapezium

1 Work out the area of these parallelograms. Remember to give the units with your answers.

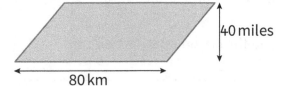

a $\frac{1}{3}$ m $\frac{1}{2}$ m

b $\frac{3}{7}$ m $\frac{5}{6}$ m

c 4 cm   65 mm

....

....

2 Work out the area of this plot of land.

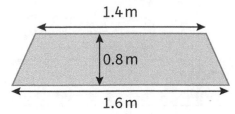

40 miles

80 km

Give your answer in:

a square kilometres

....

b square miles

....

3 Windscreen glass for a van costs $250 per square metre.

The diagram shows a van windscreen in the shape of a trapezium.

1.4 m

0.8 m

1.6 m

Work out the cost of the glass for the windscreen.

....

....

....

17.3 The area and circumference of a circle

1 You can write the area and circumference of a circle in terms of π like this:

When the radius = 5 cm   Area = $\pi r^2 = \pi \times 5^2 = 25\pi$ cm^2

Circumference = $2\pi r = 2 \times \pi \times 5 = 10\pi$ cm

Write the area and circumference of these circles in terms of π.

a Radius = 3 cm

Area = ...

Circumference = ...

b Radius = 7 cm

Area = ...

Circumference = ...

2 Circle A has a diameter of 8 cm and circle B has a diameter of 16 cm.

a Show that for circle A, the area = 16π cm^2 and the circumference = 8π cm.

....

....

b Work out the area and circumference of circle B in terms of π.

....

....

c Complete the table.

> $5\pi : 15\pi$ simplifies to $1 : 3$.

Circle A : Circle B	Radius (cm)	Circumference (cm)	Area (cm^2)
Ratio	4 : 8	8π :	16π : ......
Ratio in its simplest form	1 : 2	...... :	...... : ......

d What do you notice about the ratios of the radius and circumference of circles A and B?

....

....

....

e What do you notice about the ratios of the radius and area of circles A and B?

....

....

....

17.4 The areas of compound shapes

1 The diagram shows a rectangular piece of pastry with eight circles cut out.

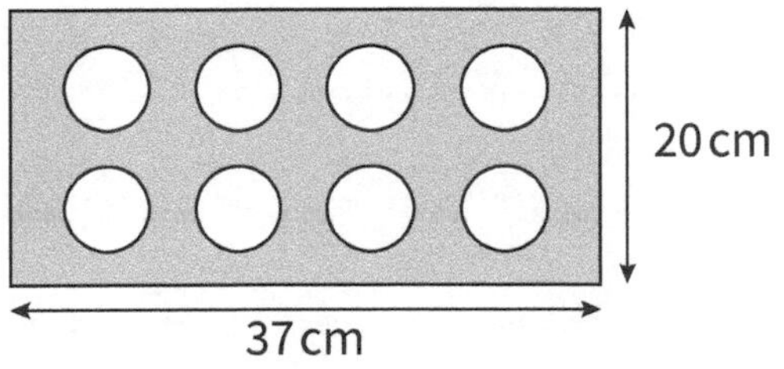

20 cm

37 cm

The diameter of each circle is 8 cm.

What is the area of the pastry that is left?

....

....

....

....

2 The diagram shows a shapes stencil.

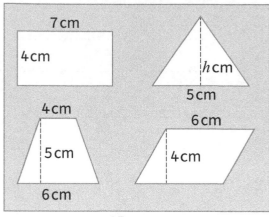

The stencil is made from a square of plastic, with the four shapes cut out.

The shaded area is 126 cm^2.

What is the height, h, of the triangle?

....

....

....

....

17.5 The volumes and surface areas of cuboids

1 The diagram shows a cuboid with a square hole cut right through it.

What is the volume of the remaining solid?

....

....

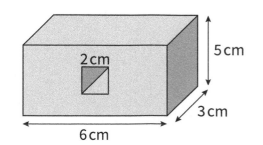

....

....

2   This cuboid has a surface area of 108 cm².

h cm

3 cm

6 cm

What is the height, h, of the cuboid?

....

....

....

....

17.6 Using nets of solids to work out surface areas

1   This square-based pyramid has a surface area of 156 cm².

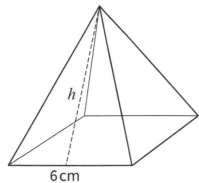

h

6 cm

What is the height, h, of the triangular faces?

....

....

....

2 Two of these triangular prisms are joined together to make a cuboid.

The areas of the faces of the triangular prism are shown in the diagram below.

back face
36 cm²

sloping face
60 cm²

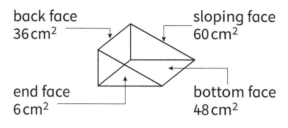

end face
6 cm²

bottom face
48 cm²

What is the surface area of the cuboid?

....

....

....

....

Mixed questions

1 There is 33 000 cm³ of water in this fish tank.

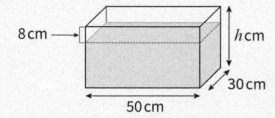

8 cm

h cm

30 cm

50 cm

What is the height, h, of the tank?

....

....

....

2 This cuboid has faces with the areas shown.

24 cm² 20 cm² 30 cm²

a What is the surface area of the cuboid?

....

....

....

....

b What is the volume of the cuboid?

Work out the dimensions of the cuboid first.

....

....

....

....

....

....

....

....

....

....

....

....

....

....

18 Interpreting and discussing results

18.1 Interpreting and drawing frequency diagrams

1 40 students were asked to text 'Happy holiday!' on a mobile phone.

The time it took them, in seconds, was recorded. The results are shown below.

10.1	11.2	9.5	7.9	12.8	4.2	17.0	9.3	24.1	13.7
5.1	3.8	12.0	10.5	15.9	14.0	11.6	7.7	9.1	12.5
13.7	15.3	11.4	5.8	10.9	23.5	6.8	14.2	18.5	14.5
11.4	22.4	6.3	10.2	16.0	14.9	12.1	17.8	8.8	16.8

a Complete the frequency table. Decide on your own class intervals.

Time to text, t (seconds)	Tally	Frequency

b Draw a frequency diagram to show the data.

18.2 Interpreting and drawing pie charts

1   The members of a gymnastics club were asked what their favourite apparatus is.

The pie chart shows the results.

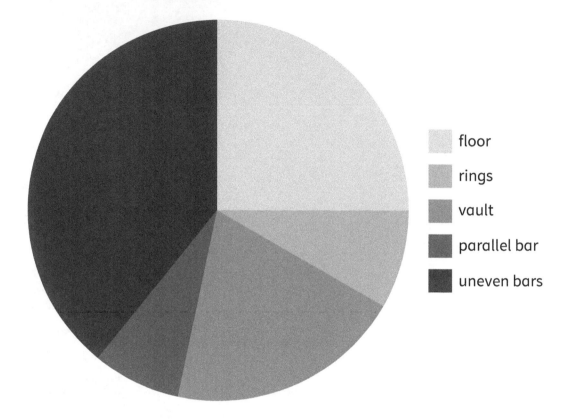

floor

rings

vault

parallel bar

uneven bars

30 members of the club chose the 'floor'.

a   How many members of the club chose:

i   the rings? ....

ii   the vault? ....

b   How many members are there altogether in the gymnastics club?

....

....

....

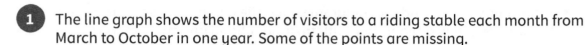

18.3 Interpreting and drawing line graphs

1 The line graph shows the number of visitors to a riding stable each month from March to October in one year. Some of the points are missing.

Complete the line graph using the information below.

July had the most visitors and March had the least. The range in the number of visitors was 29.

September had three times as many visitors as March. August had the same number as April and May added together. The ratio of visitors in April : May was 2 : 3.

June had 80% of the number of visitors in July.

The mean number of visitors per month was 25.

....

....

....

18.4 Interpreting and drawing stem-and-leaf diagrams

1 This back-to-back stem-and-leaf diagram shows the distances, to the nearest metre, that 29 students threw a tennis ball with their right hand and their left hand.

Distance thrown with left hand   Distance thrown with right hand

```
8  8  8  7  5  5  4  4  2 | 0 | 3  7  8  8
8  7  6  5  4  2  2  1  0 | 1 | 3  4  4  5  6  6  6  7  9  9
      8  4  4  3  2  1  1  0 | 2 | 0  2  3  5  5  6  8
            8  5  2 | 3 | 3  3  4  5  6  7  8  8
```

Key: 0 | 3 means 3 metres

a Complete the table below showing the data for the distances thrown.

	Least distance	Greatest distance	Range	Median distance	Mean distance	Modal distance
Right hand						
Left hand						

b Make two comments about what the data shows.

....

....

c How many students do you think are left-handed? Explain your answer.

....

....

18.5 Drawing conclusions

1. The table shows the mean monthly temperatures (°C) in Kangerlussuaq, Greenland and Port Stanley, Falkland Islands over one year. The temperatures are given to the nearest 1°C.

	Jan	Feb	Mar	Apr	May	Jun	Jul	Aug	Sep	Oct	Nov	Dec
Kangerlussuaq	−20	−21	−18	−8	3	9	11	8	3	−6	−12	−16
Port Stanley	11	10	9	7	5	3	2	3	5	7	8	10

a. On the graph below, draw a line for each set of data.

Mean monthly temperature in Kangerlussuaq and Port Stanley

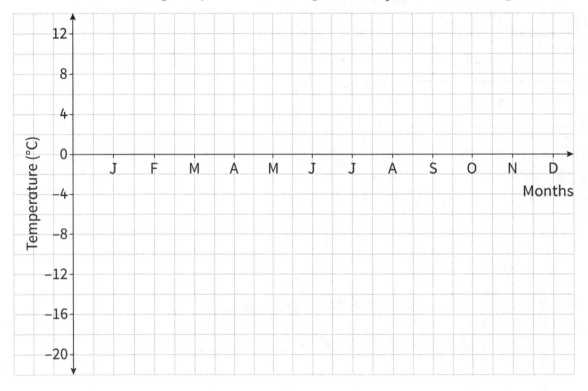

b. Write a short paragraph comparing the temperatures in Kangerlussuaq and Port Stanley. You could use words such as 'maximum', 'minimum', 'warmer', 'colder', 'variation', 'consistent'.

....

....

....

....

....

121

Mixed questions

1 The frequency table and diagram, and the stem-and-leaf diagram, all show the same information. They all show the number of emails received by employees of a company on one day.

Anders has spilt tea over the diagrams.

Number of emails received	Frequency
0–9	
10–19	
20–29	18
30–39	
40–49	
Total	60

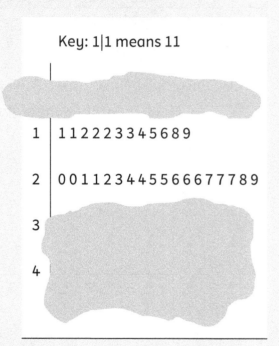

Key: 1|1 means 11

```
1 | 1 1 2 2 2 3 3 4 5 6 8 9
2 | 0 0 1 1 2 3 4 4 5 5 6 6 6 6 7 7 7 8 9
3 |
4 |
```

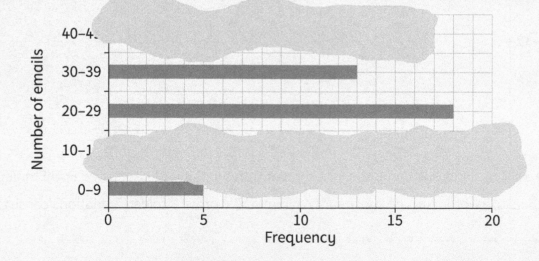

Use the information from the diagrams to draw a pie chart for the data.

Use the information to work out all the frequencies first.

....

....

....

....

....

....

Notes